Darrell Huffman

The Miracle of the Seed

Foreword by Kenneth W. Hagin

WestBow Press®
A Division of Thomas Nelson & Zondervan

WestBow Press books may be ordered through booksellers or by contacting:

WestBow Press
A Division of Thomas Nelson & Zondervan
1663 Liberty Drive
Bloomington, IN 47403
www.westbowpress.com
1 (866) 928-1240

ISBN: 978-1-4908-9104-0 (sc)
ISBN: 978-1-4908-9105-7 (hc)
ISBN: 978-1-4908-9103-3 (e)

Library of Congress Control Number: 2015910858

Print information available on the last page.

WestBow Press rev. date: 07/06/2015

Contents

Foreword

I CONSIDER IT AN HONOR to write this foreword for a man whom I consider a friend. Our relationship began over thirty-seven years ago, when Darrell became a student at Rhema Bible Training College. Through the years, I've watched his church and ministry grow and have a positive impact on the body of Christ. He challenges those who will hear to a deeper revelation of the Word of God and a more intimate relationship with God.

Darrell and I have had many opportunities to minister alongside each other at Rhema's Campmeeting, A Call to Arms, and other various events. Darrell is a dynamic minister. I hold him in high regard as a teacher of the Word. This is why I am pleased to recommend his book, *The Miracle of the Seed*. I believe it will encourage you to press on, knowing that you can't outgive God—whether it's your money, your time or your talents. This book will help you develop a lifestyle of sowing your best into the kingdom of God, so that, in turn, you'll reap a great harvest of reward all the days of your life!

—Kenneth W. Hagin
President, Kenneth Hagin Ministries
and Rhema Bible Training College,
Pastor, Rhema Bible Church

Introduction

From the beginning of creation, God set forth provision and an abundance of blessing for humanity. The method the Lord chose to bring about His provision was through the miracle of the seed.

Genesis 1:11–12 says, "Then God said, 'Let the earth bring forth grass, the herb that yields seed, and the fruit tree that yields fruit according to its kind, whose seed is in itself, on the earth'; and it was so. And the earth brought forth grass, the herb that yields seed according to its kind, and the tree that yields fruit, whose seed is in itself according to its kind. And God saw that it was good." This is the law that God set in motion upon the earth—that everything would produce fruit after its kind with seed within itself to produce the next harvest. Man was to eat the fruit and plant the seed. In following this simple law of seedtime and harvest, the provision of God would be constant in man's life. The miracle of the next harvest of blessing was in the seed.

In Genesis 8:22, we see God reaffirming this law of provision and blessing after the great flood. In verse 22, God said, "While the earth remains, seedtime and harvest, cold and heat, winter and summer, and day and night shall not cease." All of these things listed in this verse are in operation on the earth today. God's law of blessing and provision is in operation on the earth today through seedtime and harvest. No matter who you are, if you plant a seed and nurture it, it will produce for you. Within it, the seed has everything you will need, but it will not produce until you sow it into the earth. The miracle takes place when the seed is planted.

When the Lord Jesus came to redeem us back into the kingdom of God, He gave us even greater revelation of seedtime and harvest. The Lord revealed that seedtime and harvest wasn't just a natural law, but also the spiritual law that would unlock the blessings of the kingdom of God. Mark 4:26–29 says, "And He said, 'The Kingdom of God is as if a man should scatter seed on the ground, and should sleep by night and rise by day, and the seed should sprout and grow, he himself does not know how. For the earth yields crops by itself: first the blade, then the head, after that the full grain in the head. But when the grain ripens, immediately he puts in the sickle, because the harvest has come.'"

One of the greatest revelations that has brought blessing to my life is this revelation of sowing and reaping. It is the law of the kingdom of God that releases blessing and provision into our life. It works in every area of our spiritual walk. Whatever we need more of, we must first sow the seed. Whether it is love, friendship, peace, prosperity, or anything else that you need, sow the right seed and you will reap a harvest back. The miracle is in the seed, and the kingdom of God is waiting to work for you when you step out in faith and sow the seed by acting on God's Word.

Your miracle is waiting on you to sow your seed. As you read the pages to come, I pray that you will receive the revelation of sowing and reaping and begin to experience the miraculous provision God has for you. Remember, the miracle is in the seed, and it's waiting on you to activate it in your life.

chapter 1

The Miracle of the Seed

These days, whether you're buying something as small as a cell phone or digital recorder, as large as a lawnmower or refrigerator, or as expensive as a car, the merchant or online business selling the item is likely to offer an extended warranty. If you add on to your warranty by an additional two, three, four, or more years, you supposedly won't face additional replacement or repair costs during that time. Likewise, with insurance—whether it is health insurance to protect us in the event of a medical catastrophe or guaranteed issue life insurance that allows us to obtain a policy without a medical exam—everyone wants a sure thing.

It is only when the phone breaks, the refrigerator quits making ice, or the car stops running that you learn about the fine print. You thought they would replace the phone no matter what happened. But when you explain that your toddler tossed the phone in the toilet or that your teenage son ran over it in the driveway, they reply, "Oh, we're sorry." You thought the car was covered from bumper to bumper, only to discover the policy didn't quite cover *everything.* In the case of guaranteed life insurance, what many salespersons won't tell you up front is that the premiums may be four or five times higher than comparable conventional policies and it offers only a limited amount of coverage.

Life, it seems, doesn't offer the kind of ironclad guarantees that so many desperately seek. Thankfully, God's Word contains the kind of everlasting truth that has not only served mankind for thousands of years, but also will remain in effect until the second coming of Christ. It provides the kind of solid guarantees that will never break down, rust out, or expire. Eternal life insurance that will literally last forever can only be found within the pages of the Bible.

The everlasting, always reliable, foundational principles contained in Scripture enable all who put them into practice to transform their lives. Following these concepts will enable you to progress from a state of poverty to prosperity, to walk out of sickness into good health, to replace misery with joy, and to leave behind the all-too-common modern state of loneliness by achieving close relationships with others. I am not talking about the prosperity message or the "name it and claim it" doctrine that has proven so popular in years past. I am talking about the Word of God that is, as Hebrews 4:12 says, living, active, and more powerful than a double-edged sword. This is the Word that will renew your mind and make you the kind of witness who will help others see the reality of Jesus Christ.

Why is God's Word so powerful? Because it contains truths and principles that have stood the test of time. They will continue to do so far into the future, long after you and I have departed from this earth. When God makes a promise, you can rely on it coming to pass. What else would motivate a man like Noah to spend a century building an ark? Forget the fables of Hollywood. The story of Noah is just one of many examples of the power of God and His principles, which will absolutely work everywhere, every place, and every time.

When God spoke to Noah, this one solitary, faithful, dependable man literally represented the future of the human race. Noah stepped out on faith. He believed God and built an ark although he had never seen rain. Genesis 2:6 describes how, in ancient times, a mist came up from the earth and watered the ground. When God sent water to drown the human race (with the exception of Noah and his family), it was an event like nothing the world had ever seen. The depths of the earth burst open with water, and the clouds above broke loose. Despite the fact that, when God first spoke to him, Noah could not imagine the events that were to unfold, Noah acted by faith and built an ark. He saved humankind from extinction, showing how faith will always bring forth great blessings.

We can see the results of Noah's faith in the aftermath of the great flood. After the waters receded and Noah removed the covering of the ark and saw that the ground had indeed dried, he went onto the land. Taking all the animals and his family with him, Noah built an altar and offered a sacrifice that soothed God's heart and prompted Him to make this promise: "While the earth remains, seedtime and harvest, cold and heat, winter and summer, and day and night shall not cease" (Genesis 8:22).

Thousands of years later, cold and heat are still in operation—ask anyone who pants for water in the midst of a sweltering southern summer or freezes through a harsh northern winter. Those extremes illustrate the reality of summer and winter, just as the sun setting each evening and rising the next morning over a twenty-four-hour cycle demonstrates the reality of night and day. If these three things are still in operation, then so is the first item in God's promise: seedtime and harvest. Farmers will tell you they need all of these elements to have any hope of success. They can't succeed if they don't plant seed; neither can they see a harvest without some cold weather to kill the bugs followed by warm weather to grow the seed. Day and night, cool weather in spring, sunlight, and the blistering heat of summer: farmers must have all of them.

Planting and Harvest

God set all these things in motion in order to prosper us, sustain us, and make us successful. Another truth worth noting here is that this is an earth law. God put it in place to govern the earth. This law works on any continent, any country, any city street, any town, or any county. Wherever somebody applies the law, it will work because God is its author. Any time you plant a seed, you will see a harvest.

God sets this in motion during the third day of creation: "Then God said, 'Let the earth bring forth grass, the herb that yields seed, and the fruit tree that yields fruit according to its kind, whose seed is in itself, on the earth' and it was so" (Genesis 1:11). God speaks it out of His mouth. He says the earth will always respond to seed and bring a harvest. The earth has a life about it that will bring life to that seed and turn it into something even better. God says this is a law that cannot be stopped as long as the earth remains, regardless of whatever else happens.

You can visit a place that has previously suffered devastation to discover that the earth has since restored itself. Consider what happened after the Mount St. Helens eruption in southwest Washington in May of 1980. The volcanic blast turned more than two hundred square miles of lush green forests, sparkling mountain streams, and pristine lakes into an ash-covered wasteland of fallen logs, avalanche debris, and muddy hillsides. And yet, despite gloomy predictions that the region would remain barren for years, within three years, 90 percent of the original plant species there were found growing again within the blast zone. What had looked like a rocky moonscape was now sprouting grass and trees. Millions of wild animals died initially, but afterward, others migrated to the area and fed on the resurgent vegetation, insects, and other creatures.[1]

Such incredible events illustrate the power of God's laws. When He says He will bring forth the herb and the tree, God is establishing a law to enable the earth to perpetuate itself and to sustain the people He created to live on this planet. Every tree will produce the blessing of fruit; inside the fruit lies a seed that can produce another tree. One of the buzzwords of modern business, government, and education is *sustainability*, which refers to environmentally friendly operations that sustain themselves and offer economical costs of operation. How much more sustainable can you get than a tree that produces fruit with the seed to create another tree?

Adam, the first man, represents all those people who came after him, including you and me. So when God speaks to Adam and Eve in Genesis, He is speaking to all men and women. After telling them to be fruitful and multiply and subdue the earth, God says, "See, I have given you every herb that yields seed which is on the face of all the earth, and every tree whose fruit yields seed; to you it shall be for food" (Genesis 1:29).

In other words, God is saying, "I'm going to let you in on a law of the earth. I'm going to give you the authority to take the seed out of the earth, and the seed will respond to you. It will produce another plant that will produce another fruit so you can eat all the time. And Adam, I'm giving you the authority to operate in this law of seedtime and harvest. As long as you obey Me and as long as you apply this law, it will operate. Every time you eat an apple, if you take the seeds out of the apple and plant them, they will produce more trees so you can have more apples. You can replenish the entire earth with apples, oranges, and anything else you want. Just plant the seed."

Using the Seed

Despite this truth, Adam never would have expanded the garden if he had eaten all the seeds or crunched them up and scattered them around carelessly. God was telling Adam that he could enjoy every piece of fruit, but only if he first planted a seed. The earth would yield whatever seed it received. This demonstrates, in addition to seedtime and harvest, the law that every seed will produce like kind. An apple seed will not grow into an orange tree. It will produce only apples. God was saying, "As long as you operate in this law, the only time you will lack for food is if you fail to plant the seeds after you have eaten the fruit. Of everything that the tree blesses you with, part of it belongs to you, but part of it belongs to the earth. You have to put part of it back where you got it from. Don't eat the part that is supposed to go back in the ground."

We can tie this idea to the principle of God's provision. Everything comes from God. Everything He gives you includes a God part and a man part. The only way you can stop the God part from working is to eat it. But if you put His part back into Him, He will bless you. This is evident from the creation account: "The Lord God planted a garden eastward in Eden, and there He put the man whom He had formed. And out of the ground the Lord God made every tree grow that is pleasant to the sight and good for food. The tree of life was also in the midst of the garden, and the tree of the knowledge of good and evil" (Genesis 2:8–9).

Sadly, by Genesis 3, we see Adam and Eve failing miserably. Instead of obeying God, they have listened to the devil (represented by the Serpent), rebelled against God, and eaten of the fruit God specifically told them to avoid (Genesis 2:17). Then, with their eyes opened, they suddenly knew shame. They had already known good; they were already like God. When they gave in to satan's temptation to know all things, they reaped calamity and evil. The devil didn't bring anything good into the world. Sin always brings death and destruction. Devastated by sin, Adam and Eve were separated from God. In fact, they hid from Him once they recognized the impact of what they had done.

As a result, God tells the devil in Genesis 3:15 that He will create enmity between him and the woman. In other words, the woman is the devil's enemy. A woman will give birth to Jesus, the Savior of the world and the One who triumphs over death. From the moment God speaks these words, He prophesies that Jesus will be satan's enemy. Is it any wonder that satan, the diabolical enemy, does everything in his power to exploit and destroy women? The devil came up with legalism and dead religion in an effort to keep women ignorant and subservient to ungodly men—macho men who fail to understand that they are merely servants of Christ, the head of the church. Have you ever watched one of those horror flicks about a monster or a dragon and the characters always sacrifice a woman to it? King Kong didn't go chasing after a man. It's not surprising that moviemakers always show a woman being sacrificed; this reflects the devil's hatred for women.

However, there is another truth in Genesis 3:15 that makes it worth quoting the entire verse: "And I will put enmity between you and the woman, and between your seed and her Seed; he shall bruise your head, and you shall bruise His heel." Did you notice what God does? Even in bringing redemption to humankind, God uses His own law of the seed. He is telling the devil that the seed He is going to plant will bring deliverance to people and destruction to the devil. What seed? Galatians says that God made a covenant with Abraham and his Seed (meaning Jesus): "He does not say, 'And to seeds,' as of many, but as of one, 'And to your Seed,' who is Christ" (Galatians 3:16).

A Great Seed

I said earlier that seed produces after its own kind. Now, the Bible says that Jesus is the Seed of the woman who will crush satan's head and bring salvation to all people. If Jesus is God's Seed, then Jesus will produce His own kind. This means that when you make Jesus Christ your Lord, you become a new person who is no longer a slave of sin. As Paul writes, "Therefore, if anyone is in Christ, he is a new creation; old things have passed away; behold, all things have become new" (2 Corinthians 5:17). We become God's workmanship, created in Christ Jesus. We are His fruit and the Lord's harvest. This is why we are called "Christians." We are Christ-like beings reproduced after the perfect Seed of Jesus.

Another truth about seedtime and harvest is that the greatness of the seed will determine the fullness of the harvest. The better the seed, the better the harvest. God could have sent an angel to die on the cross; angels are wonderful beings who accomplish significant works. He could have created a world with streets of gold lined with jewels and used that to redeem us. But you can't get a mighty harvest out of a puny seed. Instead, He sent His greatest Seed: His Son. The greatest Seed ever planted is still reaping a perpetual harvest that will continue until the end of time. Everyone who has accepted Jesus as Savior and Lord is part of His Seed. We have God's nature because we are made in His likeness. We walk in His fullness and power. We are part of His body. We are bone of His bone and flesh of His flesh. We are of His Spirit.

Jesus Himself taught that "unless a grain of wheat falls into the ground and dies, it remains alone; but if it dies, it produces much grain" (John 12:24). He was saying that when a seed is planted, it will bring a great harvest. But we have to be willing to release it before we can get it back. We have to be willing to let it die in its present form before God can shape it into His form. And He can only give an increase when we release it into His hands. After all, God planted the very best Seed He could offer. He sowed it into the human race so He could reap a great harvest of souls for His kingdom. He operated under the same law He gave to us.

Not only did He operate under this same law during His time on earth, Jesus also initiated the law of the seed into God's kingdom. In essence, He told us, "Seedtime and harvest is not only an earth law; it's now a kingdom law. God the Father set up the earth to operate on the law of seed. Now I'm setting up the kingdom the same way. Just as a natural seed produces a harvest in any soil, anywhere, the seed of the Spirit will produce a harvest in any heart, anywhere." In the parables He taught to a multitude gathered by the sea, Jesus said, "The kingdom of God is as if a man should scatter seed on the ground, and should sleep by night and rise by day, and the seed should sprout and grow, he himself does not know how. For the earth yields crops by itself: first the blade, then the head, after that the full grain in the head. But when the grain ripens, immediately he puts in the sickle, because the harvest has come" (Mark 4:26–29).

Principles of Success

There are three principles in Mark 4:26–29 that you need to have working in your life if you hope ever to embrace prosperity, good health, happiness, and many rewarding relationships:

1. **First, you have to be a sower—an initiator and a giver.**

You have to plant seed before God can bring a harvest. The action is on the part of the sower, which is you. The response comes from God because He is a responder. We initiate in faith and God responds. Out of one Seed, God destroyed satan, triumphed over demons, demolished the power of sin, conquered death, and brought redemption to the human race. He raised up Jesus as the head of the church. Out of this perfect Seed, everyone who calls on the name of the Lord becomes a part of God's harvest. If you doubt this, you need to consider some powerful passages from Scripture:

- In speaking to His disciples, Christ says He has turned over the authority of God's kingdom to His followers: "And I will give you the keys of the kingdom of heaven, and whatever you bind on earth will be bound in heaven, and whatever you loose on earth will be loosed in heaven" (Matthew 16:19).
- Right before ascending to heaven, Jesus says, "All authority has been given to Me in heaven and on earth. Go therefore and make disciples of all the nations, baptizing them in the name of the Father and of the Son and of the Holy Spirit, teaching them to observe all things that I have commanded you" (Matthew 28:18–20).
- Mark's gospel records this final scene this way: "And He said to them, "Go into all the world and preach the gospel to every creature. He who believes and is baptized will be saved; but he who does not believe will be condemned. And these signs will follow those who believe: In My name they will cast out demons; they will speak with new tongues; they will take up serpents; and if they drink anything deadly, it will by no means hurt them; they will lay hands on the sick, and they will recover" (Mark 16:15–18).

2. ✓ **Second, for you to become a sower and a giver, God must be your source.**

There is a difference between a source and an instrument. An instrument is what God uses to bring you a blessing, but He is the source. I once heard noted Australian pastor Patsy Cameneti give a fascinating illustration of this. During a trip to the Himalayas, she talked with natives of the region who spoke of the great river, the Ganges. They said the volume of water it contained could flood all the rivers of the world. However, because of a drought, at that time the water level had sunken so low that Patsy could see rocks jutting out from the surface. She realized they were part of the riverbed. The people told her they had been in a drought. "Look up on the mountains," one of them said. "You don't see as much snow. All the water comes from snow." No sooner had this person spoken than God whispered to Patsy: "That's wrong. Look above the mountains. If the heavens don't release the right things, snow doesn't fall on the mountains. Too often people put their eyes on the wrong thing. I'm the source of the snow, which releases the water, which fills up the river, which floods the plain and brings life to the people. All great things come from Me."

You have to look beyond the mountains. You may think your job, or the well-paying position you attained through your educational and professional experience, or the handsome pension you earned after forty years of work is your source. It isn't. The economic downturn that started in late 2007 proved that jobs, investments, and other man-made sources of wealth can vanish in the twinkling of an eye. None of them is your source. You must look to the One who produces the snow that eventually allows you to eat and live.

Third, you must give yourself to God.

You will never act on God's Word and become a giver until you give yourself to God and trust Him with your life. A primary reason that too many of God's children do not give offerings, sow seeds, reach out to others, or do the other things He tells them to do is because they have never totally given themselves to Him. They may say that they trust Him, but in reality they trust more in their own efforts. If you give yourself to God and trust Him, you will trust Him as your source. When you trust Him, you will reach out to others and be a friend; trusting God will make the relationship work and enable you to become honest enough to expose the vulnerabilities in your makeup. When you trust God, you are free to love your spouse. When I trust in God, I can trust my wife and give myself completely to her, knowing she will respond to the love that originates with God.

The same is true when it comes to giving. You can only be a giver if you trust God to make something work when you sow a seed into it. People do not refrain from being givers just because they don't have any money. Various surveys have shown that anywhere from 35 to 50 percent of people who attend church give nothing to it. One research project revealed that only 3 to 5 percent of Americans tithe, although 17 percent claim to do so. Among church members of eleven leading denominations in the United States and Canada, per-member giving as a percentage of income was lower in the year 2000 than it was in 1921 or 1933 (around the time of the Great Depression.)[2]

The sad truth is that many who claim they can't afford to give *can* afford to go shopping at the mall. They can afford to go out for dinner. They can afford a new wardrobe. They can afford a new car. They can afford to see the latest movies. They give their money to all kinds of things, often because they get something in return. When you withhold your money from God's work, you have not given yourself to Him in this area. The same is true with relationships. If you were hurt in the past and now withhold yourself from other people, it is not just a sign that you will reap a lonely life. This habit also shows that you do not trust God to protect you from harm and allow you to make new friends.

If this is true of you—if you are a miser with your money, your time, and yourself—then you need to learn to trust in God. In giving to others, whether it is of money, talents, or simply prayer support, you will discover joy that lasts. You will reach that blessed state of spiritual maturity where you initiate and give because God is your source. You will have given yourself to God, and this will become evident to everyone who comes in contact with you. You will know firsthand the awesome miracle of the seed.

chapter 2

The Miracle of the Source

If money alone could buy happiness, there wouldn't be so many miserable lottery winners. We saw firsthand evidence of that one time in West Virginia, when a businessman won a multistate, multimillion-dollar Powerball jackpot, but over the next few years, reaped a series of heartaches. Other examples abound, such as the woman who won New Jersey's lottery twice but lost the entire $5.4 million and wound up living in a trailer. "I won the American dream but I lost it, too," she says. "It was a very hard fall. It's called rock bottom. Everybody wanted my money. Everybody had their hand out. I never learned one simple word in the English language—no."[1]

A man who won more than $16 million in Pennsylvania's lottery wound up existing on meager social security payments. While he still had the fortune, his former girlfriend sued him in an effort to share in his winnings, police arrested one of his brothers for hiring a hit man to kill him in hopes of inheriting some of the money, and other siblings persuaded him to invest in two failed Florida businesses. As you can imagine, all that strained the man's relationships. Eight years after a woman in Missouri won $3.1 million, she filed for bankruptcy with only $700 remaining in two bank accounts and no cash.

One certified financial planner in Florida says that for many people, such jackpots can cause disaster. "In our culture, there is a widely held belief that money solves problems," says Susan Bradley, founder of the Sudden Money Institute. "People think if they had more money, their troubles would be over. When a family receives sudden money, they frequently learn the money can cause as many problems as it solves." Craig Wallace, a senior officer with a company that advances lump sums and takes repayments from lottery winners' annuity payments, says going broke is a common malady, especially with winners of smaller amounts. "Say you've won $1 million," Wallace says. "What you've really won is a promise to be paid $50,000 a year. People win and think they're millionaires. They go out and buy houses and cars and before they know it, they're in way over their heads."[2]

These sad stories demonstrate the reality that the object of money is not to lavish it on oneself, but to use it for God's purposes, including helping others. When God is your source, you will seek His direction on how to use the blessings that He brings. As you do this, you will become a river of praise. The Lord proved His faithfulness in providing for us in the Biblical account of Abraham (then still Abram). In Genesis 15:1, He tells the patriarch of Israel that He will be Abraham's shield and his exceedingly great reward. God speaks these words after Abraham has won a fight to take back his captured nephew and given tithes to Melchizedek, the king of Salem who foreshadowed Christ. But then Abraham wonders if he has done the right thing. When God assures Abraham that he has done so, God is telling him, "I'm your source for everything. I will give you increases in pay. As long as you trust Me, you won't need men to get you through. I will do that."

Entering Covenant

When Abraham receives this word, he moves right into covenant with God. The fifteenth chapter of Genesis describes this covenant. God promises Abraham his descendants will be as numerous as the stars in the sky. This is the same promise He made to His followers in New Testament times, as expressed by the apostle Paul: "And my God shall supply all your need according to His riches in glory by Christ Jesus" (Philippians 4:19). God is telling us to look to Him for our needs, not to other people, businesses, relationships, political favors, abilities, or talents. God is not only our source; but in whatever area we completely trust God we will sow into that area, be it your church, a missionary, a ministry, or a business.

Besides trusting in God as your source, you must give

so that it may be given unto you. Jesus taught this in His parable of the growing seed (quoted in chapter 1): "And He said, 'The kingdom of God is as if a man should scatter seed on the ground, and should sleep by night and rise by day, and the seed should sprout and grow, he himself does not know how'" (Mark 4:26–27). You have to sow your seed into the ground before it can spring up and grow. God does everything through the planted seed. It isn't the seed you carry around but the seed you plant that matters.

This doesn't apply just to money. Your love will never grow until you release it. You can carry around a wealth of love in your heart, but if it is left unspoken or undemonstrated, it will simply lie there and not do anyone any good. If you desire more friends, you must start investing in other people so your love can spring up and grow. If you want to change the atmosphere in a place—for example, a business, home, or social group—commit yourself to God in that area. If you are guilty of getting caught up in the negative chorus that is so common in many settings and you have made rude or mean-spirited comments, ask God to cleanse and forgive you. Then start planting seeds of kindness and love. The off-color language in your office or other work environments may slowly slip away if you begin to express positive, caring thoughts for others instead. No matter how much the devil tries to persuade you otherwise, your influence counts.

"But they might take it the wrong way," you may protest. "They might see me as weak."

No. Meekness is not weakness. Being meek means being surrendered to God and letting Him change the atmosphere around you. Whatever you sow, God will cause it to grow. As Luke puts it: "Give, and it will be given to you: good measure, pressed down, shaken together, and running over will be put into your bosom. For with the same measure that you use, it will be measured back to you" (Luke 6:38). In other words, what you sow is what will come back to you. If you give out love, you will receive love in return. If you give generously to your church or to another person, God will give back to you. He will even expand it. As Matthew 13:8 and Mark 4:20 say, the increase may be thirtyfold, sixtyfold, or a hundredfold. The size of your seed will determine the size of your harvest.

This teaching continues in 2 Corinthians, where Paul writes, "Now may He who supplies seed to the sower, and bread for food, supply and multiply the seed you have sown and increase the fruits of your righteousness, while you are enriched in everything for all liberality, which causes thanksgiving through us to God" (2 Corinthians 9:10–11). God not only brings growth to your seed, He also gives you the seed in the first place! Since God gives everyone some kind of seed, you need to search for yours. Once you find it, plant it. Let's return to the example of an apple. In its original state, you won't find any seed in it. Have you ever bit into one and missed the seed because you gnawed it all the way to the core? You weren't paying any attention to the seed; you just devoured the whole thing.

We can be like picnickers on the Fourth of July who eat a slice of watermelon and miss the seeds. When I was a kid and we went to my grandparents' house in the country, we would sit on their porch and eat watermelon, spitting out the seeds. Too many people either spit out the seeds or consume them and then toss the rind over the hill for God. If instead you take those seeds and plant them, you will have a watermelon patch the next summer. This same principle applies to your giving. You have to give something if you expect to see a harvest.

Expect a Miracle

Once you have recognized God as your source and you give generously, the third thing you must do is expect a miracle. Jesus taught in the parable of the growing seed: "But when the grain ripens, immediately he puts in the sickle, because the harvest has come" (Mark 4:29). If you trust God and act on what He said, you can trust Him to do what He said. You can expect healing, friends, and your bills getting paid on time—not because of some kind of magic trick, but because of the law of seedtime and harvest. You can expect God to do what He said He would.

Friends in particular are a crying need for many in the twenty-first century. With social media, smartphones, and the Internet everywhere we go, many become lost in a morass of electronic communication. It appears that we have hundreds of friends, all accessible at the touch of a finger. But the reality is that few people have more than one friend or two upon whom they can count in the midst of calamity, death, or other great loss. Many comments on Facebook don't come from people whose shoulders you can cry on or who you can later look in the eye.

Now, when I say you should show yourself to be friendly, please recognize that there is a difference between showing yourself friendly and acting like a bozo. I compare this to dumping a whole handful of seeds into one hole. When the crop starts coming up, it will be a mess. Sow your seed wisely and intelligently. If you sow in thorns, it won't work. The same goes for rocks. However, if you find some good people in whom to sow seeds of friendship, then planting those seeds will bring you a healthy return. Right now, if you're in the grips of loneliness and shattered relationships, this may sound impossible. But when you sow, you need to expect a miracle. Realize that God takes nothing and makes it into something.

Remember, though, that you can't expect to see a miracle if you don't plant anything. No harvest comes when there is no seed. I have heard people exclaim that God will meet all of their needs, yet they don't put any seed in the ground. Nothing will come from nothing. If you sow nothing, you get nothing back. At the beginning of the journey, it can be discouraging to feel like you're standing in a field with nothing but a few dried-up old apples to provide some seeds. You wonder how such a meager supply could lead to any kind of harvest. You may not have any tools for plowing the ground. If that is the case, scratch and dig with your hands and feet; do whatever you have to do to get some seed planted.

In modern times, too many people expect to see a great return from very little effort on their part. That isn't what God told Adam and Eve. One of the consequences of their disobedience was strenuous toil: "In the sweat of your face you shall eat bread till you return to the ground, for out of it you were taken; for dust you are, and to dust you shall return" (Genesis 3:19). In other words, life will get tough now and then. Getting your seed into the ground takes sweat. You may have to sacrifice, put in long hours, and go to a whole new level of trusting God. Still, the Lord set the law of seedtime and harvest in motion in His kingdom. If you plant seed, you can expect Him to increase it.

In practical terms, that means that if you stay in the same church for a while, you will be blessed. Every church has its flaws and shortcomings, disappointments and trials, and yet it is still God's instrument for overcoming satan. If you quit jumping from place to place or having a falling-out every time you face the least disagreement, you will reap the love and rewards of long-term relationships. Likewise, if you keep reading your Bible, you will receive God's wisdom and guidance instead of relying on mankind's latest whim. If you keep praising God, you will see more reasons to praise Him. Stay put and let God do what He said He would do.

Wait on the Harvest

Some people never see a harvest because they quit before God can bring it to them. If God told you what to do and didn't tell you to do anything else, then keep doing what He told you to do. It will work. Expect a miracle. If God said it, you can believe it. This is what Paul wrote about in his first letter to the church at Corinth: "I planted, Apollos watered, but God gave the increase" (1 Corinthians 3:6). If you plant it, God will increase it. This takes trust, so if your faith has faltered lately, recognize your need to return to that state of faith in which you believe that God is your Father and that He does reward His children.

Whether what you need is financial help, healing, or reconciliation with friends or loved ones, get some seed into the ground. When the harvest comes, do what Jesus taught in Mark 4:29 and put in the sickle. A sickle is a threshing instrument. In Ephesians 6:17, Paul says the sword of the Spirit is God's Word. *Sword* here means instrument of cutting or attacking and *word* means rhema, or an utterance of God. So we could say that the sword of the Spirit—the threshing instrument of the Holy Ghost—is a confession of the Word.

Speaking is important because the way that you will see your miracle is with your mouth. Confess your harvest.

Confess an abundance of friends who are faithful, loyal, true, and will never let you down. If you have sown yourself into others, God will bring an abundant harvest of friends. If you have sown for financial needs through your tithes and offerings, thank God that He will bring you enough to meet every financial need in your life. Thank Him for bringing you a harvest of success. Confess the miracle before it materializes. Live with the awareness that the harvest is coming.

This is why all farmers go out and plow their fields in the spring. They get the soil ready and plant their seeds, expecting to reap a harvest in the fall. They can depend upon this because of the law of seedtime and harvest that God established in Genesis 8:22. Before this harvest comes, farmers can expect to endure blistering heat on some days and too much rain on others. They will have to get out there and pluck out weeds or chase away pests and vermin trying to steal their crops before they are ripe. They will have to work the field and protect it from bugs and other hazards. But when that harvest comes in, a farmer won't sit there and recall the wind, rain, sun, and heat. He will brag about his harvest, saying, "I'm telling you, I got the biggest harvest I've ever had from this plot of ground. I brought in more produce this year than I did in the past five put together."

Likewise, when you are healed, you won't talk about the days you spent praying, speaking the Word, or meditating on Scripture as you cried out to God in the midst of aches and pains. You will stand up and say, "It's so good to be healed. I'm so glad God healed me. I sowed my faith into God and He healed my body. I'm whole, in Jesus' name. Hallelujah!"

Sacrificial Giving

My wife, Bonnie, and I can recite story after story of how we sacrificed so we could be tithers and givers. When we were first married, we attended a church near the campus of the college where I played football. The pastor of that church served as the team chaplain, and during and after games, we chatted and formed a relationship. One evening, he visited us at our postage stamp–sized apartment and shared with us about the wisdom of tithing. Not having much knowledge of spiritual things at the time, I didn't know what tithing was. He told us it meant giving 10 percent of our income to God as an act of worship, and also spreading the gospel to others. He gave us some tithing envelopes with Malachi 3:10 printed on them, telling us to trust God and give. That sparked our lifelong practice of sowing our tithe into our local church. It wasn't much, but we made sure it was 10 percent.

This teaching became particularly significant one weekend when we didn't know where to turn to for our next meal. That Friday evening, we had no money, no gas in our car, and barely any food in our apartment. We finally scrounged up four slices of white bread and some sandwich meat. We made two sandwiches and poured a glass of water for each of us. As we prayed over our meal, we thanked the Lord for it and asked Him to help us through the weekend. After our meager dinner, I prayed alone. I reminded the Lord that we were His children, that we were committed to Him, and that, no matter what, we would never turn from Him. I then requested for Him to help us through, reminding Him that in Malachi 3:10–11, His Word said that He would open the heavens and bless us. I concluded by thanking Him and putting it in His hands.

About two hours later, Bonnie's four sisters showed up at our apartment for a surprise visit. Each one carried a bag of groceries in her arms. Although they didn't know our cupboards were literally bare, they had just decided to bring us some groceries that evening. God had supernaturally supplied our need! From that day to this one, we have never again lacked food or provisions. We have tithed, trusted God, and stayed steady. The Lord has proved Himself greater than our need.

Trusting in God

I am so glad that Bonnie and I learned the value of putting our trust in God early in our married life. During the years immediately following our miraculous grocery delivery, the Lord called me into ministry. Besides playing football and keeping up my studies, I worked in the church as a youth pastor during my junior and senior years. After graduation, we moved back to Virginia, where Bonnie grew up. While working at my job, I searched for the right Bible school to continue my education. If I was going to be able to preach and to help people, I knew I needed more training in the Word of God. There were several Bible schools near our home, so I planned to continue working while attending classes.

However, as we prayed for direction, we discovered that the Lord had other plans for us. Through some miraculous events, He led us to consider a small Bible college in Oklahoma. This was in June, school started in September, and the school happened to be fourteen hours away from where we lived. Despite the obstacles, I got an application, sent it in, and received my acceptance letter in the first week of August. The problem was that when I received the acceptance letter, we had only thirty dollars in our savings account. We added everything up and calculated that for me to attend this school, we would need twelve hundred dollars! That may not seem like much today, but in 1977 this goal looked like an unmovable object, that mountain Jesus talked about in Mark 11:23—especially to a young college-age couple still preparing for their life's calling.

Bonnie and I discussed ways we could come up with the money and we set our faith to believing God. One day, while I was in prayer, a thought came to me: *Why not hold back your tithe? After all, you would be using the money for the work of the Lord.* As I thought about this,

I remembered that the Word says the tithe is holy and belongs to God. I knew in my heart that this thought to hold back my tithe didn't come from God. Taking on the appearance of the angel of light of which Paul wrote about in 2 Corinthians 11:14, the devil was hoping to persuade me to divert my tithe. I realized that satan was trying to stop me from sowing my seed to prevent my seeing God meet our need.

Fortunately, I had learned enough to know that we are to sow the tithe into God's storehouse, no matter what. No matter how good the cause, it is never our right to use this money for ourselves. So Bonnie and I prayed. Afterward, we decided that we would not only tithe, but also add a little extra as an act of faith that God would supply our need. The next few weeks were tough. When it came time to leave for Oklahoma, we counted up our funds. We had twelve hundred and fifty dollars! God had again proven that if we put our trust in Him and sow our seed, He will meet our need.

Now, when we share these kinds of stories, we don't lament the hard luck we endured or the sad moments when discouragement set in, nor do we describe all our struggles. We talk about how God turned things around and brought in what we were believing Him for. We kept our eyes on the harvest, not the battle. Farmers don't keep their eyes on the bugs, the heat, the rain, or the wind. They keep their eyes on the harvest.

So, what harvest are you believing God for today?

chapter 3

Don't Dig Up Your Seed

In December of 2013, a federal grand jury in Iowa indicted six Chinese nationals for allegedly plotting to steal bio-engineered corn seed from US companies. The thieves reportedly went as far as to dig it up from test fields and send it to conglomerates in China. The twenty-one page indictment handed up in Des Moines claimed that the Chinese drove through rural areas of Iowa, Illinois, and Indiana to dig up freshly planted seed or to collect grown corn to obtain samples of this stock. The seeds represented years of work and millions of dollars in research and development. One company affected by the loss of a particular line of seed said it could cost them $30 million to $40 million and wipe out more than five years of research.

The Christian Science Monitor reported that the investigation started in May of 2011 after a seed company's field manager noticed an Asian man on his knees in a freshly planted cornfield while another waited nearby in a car. This happened in an unmarked test plot in a rural area of Iowa. Agents suspected the Chinese received inside information regarding the secret location of the plot from someone working in one of the companies. The Asian man claimed to be from the University of Iowa and said that he would be attending an upcoming agricultural conference in the state, but the project manager recorded the car's license number. Federal agents later traced it to a Chinese businessman in South Florida. Among those charged was Mo Hailong of Boca Raton, Florida, who was described as the international business director of the Beijing Dabeinong Technology Group Company—part of a Chinese conglomerate with a corn seed subsidiary.[1]

This is an admittedly extreme example of the damage that can occur from digging up seed. Nevertheless, it illustrates a significant spiritual truth: Never dig up the seed of God's Word. It needs time to grow in your spirit. You need constant reading, study, memorization, and meditation to accomplish this task. This is serious stuff, but a recent survey by respected demographer George Barna shows that, despite a proliferation of printed and electronic Bibles in our country, only a minority of Americans actually read them. The Barna Group found that, while 80 percent of respondents believe the Bible is holy or sacred literature, fewer than half admit to reading it more than a couple of times a year. "The typical American actually has 4.7 Bibles, yet only 37 percent of

Americans use the Bible in a typical month," says Barna Group president David Kinnaman. "So we have a huge gap between awareness, presentation, and usage of Scripture."[2]

It is obvious that millions of people fail to appreciate the Word's value. God calls the Word seed—not just any seed, but "incorruptible" seed, as shown by Peter's first letter to the church in Asia Minor: "Being born again, not of corruptible seed, but of incorruptible, by the word of God, which liveth and abideth for ever" (1 Peter 1:23 KJV). In addition to the perfect Seed of Christ, the Word is another perfect seed that helps bring you into the kingdom of God. It lives and reigns forever. The Word of God is living seed, alive with everything that Scripture says and teaches. Its very name is an expression of what it contains. It is similar to what I often hear expressed at springtime: "I'm gonna plant some tomato seeds." The tomato seed will produce tomatoes. The Word of God will produce all kinds of good things, such as healing.

In the second chapter of 1 Peter, the apostle writes that God called us to follow Jesus because "Christ also suffered for us, leaving us an example, that you should follow His steps: 'Who committed no sin, nor was deceit found in His mouth'; who, when He was reviled, did not revile in return; when He suffered, He did not threaten, but committed Himself to Him who judges righteously; who Himself bore our sins in His own body on the tree, that we, having died to sins, might live for righteousness—by whose stripes you were healed" (1 Peter 2:21–24). The last phrase of this passage describes the healing in that seed, which God already called incorruptible. In other words, the seed of this Word will save you and heal you if you will plant it in your heart.

The Seed of Life

Everything that lives began as a seed. Even a mighty oak tree, which can reach seventy feet in height and nine feet (or more) in width, starts as a seemingly insignificant acorn. Everything in the oak started in that seed. Every bit of its thick bark, colorful leaves, and majestic branches came from that acorn. If you plant a seed, you will get a tree. The same seed that produces mighty results in the natural also produces impressive results in the supernatural.

No one should ever discount the power of the seed of God's Word. When Paul wrote his letter to the church at Philippi, he noted that in the jail where he was confined, it had become obvious that his faith had led to his arrest. That inspired many of his brethren to become bolder in their preaching. And yet, at the same time, others preached from a contentious spirit: "Some indeed preach Christ even from envy and strife, and some also from goodwill: The former preach Christ from selfish ambition, not sincerely, supposing to add affliction to my chains; but the latter out of love, knowing that I am appointed for the defense of the gospel" (Philippians 1:15–18).

So, in spite of the encouragement and support of some, did the opposition Paul faced disturb him? Not in the least. For the apostle, no matter what the motive of those speaking the Word, he appreciated how each person was spreading the gospel: "What then? Only that in every way, whether in pretense or in truth, Christ is preached; and in this I rejoice, yes, and will rejoice" (Philippians 1:19). When this seed is released, it will produce life and goodness and last longer than a two-hundred-year-old oak tree. The Word of God will never lose its strength or its ability. Some seeds will dry out, lose their vigor, and no longer produce. You can take the Word of God, set it on a shelf, and walk away. But if you come back ten years later, pull it off the shelf, and act on it, it will still work. It will work at any time, at any stage of your life, and in any situation.

It doesn't matter how long your battle rages. The Word will still be alive if you stay with it. It is an incorruptible seed and full of life because it describes God's Word and what He wants to do for you. Plant the seed and watch it work. This is the truth the prophet Isaiah expressed in his book. One of the most powerful passages in all of Scripture appears in the chapter 55, when God speaks these words through Isaiah: "'For My thoughts are not your thoughts, nor are your ways My ways,' says the Lord. 'For as the heavens are higher than the earth, so are My ways higher than your ways, and My thoughts than your thoughts. For as the rain comes down, and the snow from heaven, and do not return there, but water the earth, and make it bring forth and bud, that it may give seed to the sower and bread to the eater, so shall My word be that goes forth from My mouth; it shall not return to Me void, but it shall accomplish what I please, and it shall prosper in the thing for which I sent it'" (Isaiah 55:8–11).

Did you catch the significance of God's comparison of the Word to rain? In other words, the Lord is saying, "Just as, when it rains and water pours out upon the ground, the rain causes a reaction on the earth, so shall the Word that goes out of My mouth do. It is just like rain. When you pour it out and plant it in yourself and others, you will get a reaction in the same way rain does." I like the way the Amplified Bible phrases the first part of verse 11: "So shall My word be that goes forth out of My mouth: it shall not return to Me void [without producing any effect, useless]." You may not think God is at work in your life, but you can rest assured that, when you plant the seed of His Word, you will see a yield.

Defeated Christians

Judging by my interaction with defeated Christians, too many fail to plant the Word and expect a harvest. You can carry your Bible around everywhere and use it so much that you wear the cover out and leave the pages fraying at the edges, yet still be defeated. I remember a man who tossed his Bible on the floor one day and jumped on it with both feet as he declared, "I'm standing on the Word." He still got his head knocked off. Literally standing on Scripture will not secure you victory. Unless the Word goes down into your heart and your spirit, it can't yield any fruit.

On one occasion, after a contentious showdown with religious leaders who complained about His teaching, Jesus tells the disciples, "It is the Spirit who gives life; the flesh profits nothing. The words that I speak to you are spirit, and they are life" (John 6:63).

In other words, His words are spiritual seeds that operate in the spiritual realm and produce results in the natural realm. God's Word is not void of power; it has the ability to produce change. However, it needs to be directed to the place where change is needed. This is how it can accomplish God's purpose. He doesn't scatter His Word around aimlessly like He's shooting a shotgun; He uses a rifle with a scope on it, zeroes in on His target, and issues a specific shot.

Too many people proclaim they believe God, but when I ask what they are believing for, they reply, "Well, whatever He wants to give me." If I ask whether they expect to be healed, and why, some will say that it is in the Bible ... "Uh, somewhere in the New Testament. I can remember reading it." If you gave that kind of statement in a courtroom, without any facts, insights, or details, you would get kicked off the witness stand. The judge would say, "We can't use your testimony."

Now, if a court official summoned you to testify, you would likely take the order pretty seriously. Well, guess what? You face a devil who is a thief, whose sole purpose is (as John 10:10 says) to steal, kill, and destroy. Revelation 12:10 calls him "the accuser of our brethren." That means he is taking your case before God every day, pleading his distorted arguments against you as he seeks to do everything possible to get your testimony thrown out of court. We must understand that if we expect God to rule in our favor, we have to cite God the facts from His Word.

We have to send out the Word and speak the Word. When we stand up to declare that we believe something, we will have to tell God *why* we believe it. We need to remind Him that He said, "I, even I, am He who blots out your transgressions for My own sake; and I will not remember your sins. Put Me in remembrance; let us contend together; state your case, that you may be acquitted" (Isaiah 43:25–26). We have to put God in remembrance because He is the judge of the highest court. He must rule between satan and me. He wants to rule in my favor, but I have to give Him something to rule with. I have to take that Word and apply it to the situation.

The devil won't quit just because you spout a few clichés or pout your lips and declare that you're mad at him. When the seven sons of the Jewish priest, Sceva, tried to cast out a demon without knowing the source of Paul's power and authority, the evil spirit replied, "Jesus I know, and Paul I know; but who are you?" (Acts 19:15).

Then the demon-possessed man overpowered all seven men and whipped them so badly that they fled from the house naked and wounded. You'd better know the Word and the Savior who personifies this Word if you expect to defeat the devil! The good thing is he *has* to obey the Word of God and the name of Jesus. He *has* to obey the truth God has spoken in His Word.

Sticking with the Word

If we want to see change in our lives, we have to plant the Word in whatever situation we want changed. The Word becomes seed and works for us. It is the most reliable tool at your disposal. How do I know this? Because Paul says in Romans: "For the gifts and the calling of God are irrevocable" (Romans 11:29). Paul was talking about the children of Israel, but we have the right to use this on our own behalf. If God caused something to happen years ago, we know He hasn't changed his mind since then.

In the full context of the passage, Paul is saying, "Though the children of God are falling away from God at this moment in time, God hasn't changed His mind about them. He still loves them. He still has a calling for them. He's going to save them in the end, when Jesus comes back." The Amplified Bible version expounds on verse 29 this way: "For God's gifts and His call are irrevocable. [He never withdraws them when once they are given, and He does not change His mind about those to whom He gives His grace or to whom He sends His call.]" What this means is that if you backslide, God simply puts His gifts and call on the shelf. The moment you repent and go back to Him, they return.

This is what *irrevocable* means. God never withdraws His gifts and calling once He gives them, and He does not change His mind about those to whom He gives His grace or to whom He issues a call. Unlike people and their often fickle, unpredictable ways, God does not change His mind. He does not waver. He is not double-minded. He does not change directions and make another decision because of adversity, circumstances, or sudden reversals of fortune. He says, "Here's the way I work. My ways are higher than your ways. My thoughts are higher than your thoughts. If you're going to operate in the way I want you to operate, you have to start thinking like I think and get up to where I am."

Not only do you have to be specific with the Word, you must also realize that, once you make a decision, you can't alter it. You have to decide, "This is the way it's going to be, whatever comes my way. I'm going to stick with the Word of God. I'm going through this obstacle." You need to reflect God's character. Even when the children of Israel rebelled and complained about their trip through the wilderness, He didn't change His mind about leading them to Canaan's land. He was still going to do it, even if he had to wait three or four generations for the grumblers to disappear.

This is what you must understand. If we expect to see God's results, we have to do as God does. What He is saying in Romans 11 is: "I never dig my seed up once it's planted. It stays in the ground. It will stay where I sent it and it will produce what I sent it to do. I don't change my mind about it. I don't decide to plant it somewhere else. I don't decide to plow it under and try something new. I choose to do what I decided to do in the first place."

Too many times, we plant a seed, but when tough circumstances arise or difficult situations come up, we waffle in our decision. When we change what we set out to do, we are digging up our seed. Seed must be left in the ground before it will work. This is why James said that we must "ask in faith, with no doubting, for he who doubts is like a wave of the sea driven and tossed by the wind. For let not that man suppose that he will receive anything from the Lord; he is a double-minded man, unstable in all his ways" (James 1:6–8).

Standing Tall

What this means is that, if you're going to rely on the Word, then you mustn't get into the Word but when things get tough, go looking for another solution. If you're going to praise God, praise God no matter what happens, no matter what challenges arise, and no matter how bleak things appear. Praise God until He carries you through to the other side. If you are going to stay true to your decision, you will have to get serious. Also, recognize that God never does anything without first making up His mind. When He spoke to Abraham in Genesis 17:4 and called him "a father of many nations," He had decided what He would do.

The Bible says Abraham then became fully persuaded that God would do what He said He would. Abraham got to a place where he said, "I don't care how old I am. I'm going to trust God. I don't care how bad I look or how old my wife is. I don't care how old she looks. If God said it, I believe it, so we are going to go ahead and act like it." And so he did. He didn't care what people said about him or what tales went around. Because of his strong faith, he could give praise to God. Can you imagine this nearly one-hundred-year-old man parading up and down the road, praising God for the coming miracle? "Hello, my name is Abraham. I'm the father of many nations."

I can envision the younger folks he encountered nodding. "Sure. Old fool. He doesn't even have one kid yet and he's calling himself the father of many nations. Have you seen Sarah lately? She was a good-looking woman back in the day, and she's still cute, but c'mon. Ninety years old is ninety years old, son."

We can get crazy thoughts in our minds and think that just because people had longer life expectancies in that era, ninety years old back then looked better than ninety years old today. Not true. And a hundred-year-old man who walked everywhere and lived a rugged lifestyle may have been stout, but I doubt he could do that many push-ups or chin-ups. I doubt he could outrun many warriors. He wouldn't have been going into many battles any longer.

Listing all the reasons and circumstances and factors behind the impossibility of God performing a miracle will kill your faith. Praise God that Abraham got fired up enough to believe God. He stood his ground for years, believing in the promise. God's Word is everlasting. Granted, he did make a mistake by trying to press the issue and having a son with Sarah's maid (a mistake that we are still paying for.) Yet when Abraham returned to faith, God's promise was still there, waiting for him.

The same is true today. Your blessing is still waiting on you. Your healing is still there. Your deliverance is ready. Whatever you are waiting for, remember that the solution lies in the seed. But if you have dug it up, then you must get it back in the ground—today! Plant the Word back into that situation so life can be brought to it. The Word will save you, heal you, deliver you, bring you peace, and fill you with the Holy Spirit. It will cause you to be an overcomer. It will turn things around and change them, just as rain changes dirt and makes it yield crops. I don't care how dry the ground is; rain is more powerful. Get enough rain in one place and the dirt will surrender.

Likewise, if you put enough Word into your situation, it will surrender. Plant that seed, keep it in the ground, and refuse to dig it up with doubt and unbelief—and it will work.

chapter 4

Operating by God's Rules

Driving abroad can get you killed if you don't know the rules of the highways. According to Advanced Drivers of America (ADA), every year an estimated 25,000 people die in road accidents abroad while they are either working or on vacation. This is why the ADA recommends such tips as carrying first aid supplies and ensuring that at least two fellow travelers know how to use them. It also advises searching the Internet prior to departing for official documents about road safety in the country where you will be traveling and thoroughly checking over rental cars or other vehicles for any visible flaws or defects before driving them on foreign roads.

"[A] significant problem for overseas visitors actually comes in two parts," says ADA President Eddie Wren. "First, they generally do not know the relevant traffic laws and regulations of the country they are visiting, and secondly, the 'traffic culture' can be very different, too. This is in addition to whether or not the relevant traffic laws are properly enforced and are, therefore, even obeyed. Pedestrian crossings [and] crosswalks, for example, may be thought of as an unbreakable rule in some countries, a mere suggestion in other countries, and a bad joke in yet other countries. On the traffic culture front, even something as simple as a pedestrian making eye contact with a driver while crossing the road can have a very different meaning and a potentially dangerous outcome."[1] Having traveled overseas, I know the truth of such statements. On one mission trip to Singapore and Thailand, it didn't take long to see that the rules of the road in those nations are much different from those in the United States. I guess because of the past influence of the British in that part of the world, drivers use what I call the "wrong" side of the road; they drive down the left side of the highway and the steering wheel is placed on the right side of the vehicle. While this practice is common in about a third of the world, to me it feels disorienting and leaves me shaking my head. I quickly noticed the difference when our missionary host came to pick us up one morning at our hotel. I saw that the traffic laws of Singapore didn't follow those in my country. Needless to say, it felt pretty weird. If I had gone over there with an American car and tried to operate it using America's road rules, I would have caused a lot of damage—and it would have been my fault.

When we reached Thailand, although the pastor

escorting us around the countryside had grown up in Oklahoma City, he had adapted to conditions in the Far East. He told me that he generally did okay on visits back to his home state—except, that is, for the time he got up at 5:00 a.m. for a long drive across Oklahoma. "I was going down this little two-lane road with no traffic," he recalled. "When there's traffic, you just automatically flow with it, but this morning there wasn't any. So I took off, driving down the wrong side of the road like I would in Thailand. Suddenly along comes this guy, driving in my lane. By this time it's six o'clock and the sun is coming up. But I start flashing my lights, thinking, *Come on, you silly thing, you're on the wrong side of the road!* That is, until I thought it over for a moment and realized that I was on the wrong side. So I swerved real quick. As he went by, blowing his horn, he looked at me like he thought, *You know, you're nuts.*"

Operating by the rules of Singapore or Thailand will work for you over there, but it will get you killed over here. You have to know where you are and what laws are at work in that particular place.

Kingdom Rules

Just like the laws governing motor vehicles, God's kingdom operates by certain rules. Jesus explained this in the parable of the seed sower, which I mentioned in chapter 2. It bears repeating here. "And He said, 'The kingdom of God is as if a man should scatter seed on the ground'" (Mark 4:26).

Christ starts this passage of teaching about God's kingdom in verse 14, saying that the sower sows the word, but the devil comes along and tries to steal it. Some people don't allow the Word to take root, and so they fall away, while others stumble because of troubles or persecution. Then there are those who allow the daily cares of life, the deceitfulness of worldly riches, or desires for fame, personal achievement, etc. to choke the Word out of their life. As a result, the seed doesn't bear any fruit.

Some describe this falling away as *backsliding.* While spiritual warfare makes this a serious problem all over the world, I believe it is particularly troublesome in affluent societies like the United States. We are saturated with modern conveniences and never-ending advertisements for consumer goods, luxury vacations, fancy cars, and other things that will supposedly offer personal fulfilment. I call it the orbit of materialism. It is easy to take our eye off the ball and let the devil snatch up the seed.

However, we should remember that, even in much simpler times, satan warred against those who proclaimed Jesus as their Lord. This happened to the first-century church at Galatia, where some believers had resorted to emphasizing the necessity of circumcision and keeping the law in order to draw close to God. That prompted Paul to write in his letter to the Galatians, "I marvel that you are turning away so soon from Him who called you in the grace of Christ, to a different gospel, which is not another; but there are some who trouble you and want to pervert the gospel of Christ. But even if we, or an angel from heaven, preach any other gospel to you than what we have preached to you, let him be accursed" (Galatians 1:4–8).

The good news here is that, despite the fact that some allowed outside forces and influences to choke the Word out of their life, Jesus taught that those who hear the Word and plant it in their hearts will bear fruit, "some thirtyfold, some sixty, and some a hundred" (Mark 4:20). Then, after reviewing another lesson about the need to let our light shine, Jesus preached verse 26: "So is the kingdom of God."

In other words, everything in God's kingdom works like this. He is saying, "If you want to see results from God, here's how you get them. Whatever you need, sow the seed." The seed is the Word of God. The ground is your situation. If you need healing, sow healing into that situation. Sow healing Scriptures into it and keep them there. Don't change your mind and dig them up. Don't withdraw them once you have sown them. Don't doubt, waver, or waffle when things get tough, or you won't be able to see any light in the tunnel.

If you are seeking prosperity, it won't come just from throwing a few dollars into the offering bucket. It comes when you get the revelation of God deep down in your spirit and believe that He will provide for all of your needs. He will even bring you blessings—not so you can lavish them upon yourself, but so you can turn around and be a blessing to others. Get rid of doubt and unbelief. Get rid of a poverty mindset, which causes people to constantly stew and fret about money and think there will never be enough. This outlook breeds fear and greed, keeping people from parting with even one dollar because they "might need it." You need to get rid of the junk that has held you in bondage and see yourself according to the Word; see yourself as successful, victorious, and prosperous. Sow your seed and get results.

If you don't know Jesus but want to be born again, apply Romans 10:8–10 to your heart: "'The word is near you, in your mouth and in your heart' (that is, the word of faith which we preach): that if you confess with your mouth the Lord Jesus and believe in your heart that God has raised Him from the dead, you will be saved. For with the heart one believes unto righteousness, and with the mouth confession is made unto salvation." Believe in your heart that Jesus died for you and God raised Him from the dead. Confess Him as Lord and you shall be saved.

Or, if you are seeking the baptism of the Holy Spirit, apply John 7:37–39: "Jesus stood and cried out, saying, 'If anyone thirsts, let him come to Me and drink. He who believes in Me, as the Scripture has said, out of his heart will flow rivers of living water.' But this He spoke concerning the Spirit, whom those believing in Him would receive; for the Holy Spirit was not yet given, because Jesus was not yet glorified." Plant that Word in yourself and the first thing you know, you will be filled with the Spirit and start speaking in tongues, no matter what your religious background or denomination. Planting the Word in the soil of your heart will yield results. Regardless of the excesses you have heard about or the critics of charismatics that thrive in some segments of the church, life in the Spirit is rich and fulfilling. It is unlike life lived in the power of human wisdom, strength, and reasoning.

Now, after you have sown the seed in the ground, you "should sleep by night and rise by day, and the seed should sprout and grow, he himself does not know how. For the earth yields crops by itself: first the blade, then the head, after that the full grain in the head" (Mark 4:27–28). Then what? In verse 29, Jesus adds, "But when the grain ripens, immediately he puts in the sickle, because the harvest has come."

God's message here is clear: "When you operate in the principles of My kingdom, you are working with Me. Your part is to speak the Word into your life. After you sow the Word into that situation, trust in Me to make it grow. Don't sweat it. Don't lose any sleep over it. Don't try to make it happen yourself. Just sow the Word, speak the Word, and believe in the Word."

Remember that life is in the Word. God cares about it so much that He watches over it to make things happen for His children.

Looking to God

The point of God's teaching is to get our eyes off the problem and onto Him so that we can enjoy life. Our part is to say it and receive it. God's part is to make it happen. Don't dig up your seed through confessions of doubt, worry, anxiety, fear, or by endlessly repeating the symptoms you are experiencing. Now, I don't mean that you should try to deny that they exist, but neither should you rehearse them and wallow in them. Praise God and believe He will remove those symptoms. Confess His Word. If someone asks you how you feel, tell them, "Don't ask me how I feel because you'll get a negative confession. Ask me what I believe. I don't want to confess my feelings. I want to confess my faith. Faith is what will put me over the top."

However, even when you speak positive words, it won't necessarily deter those who want to see bad things and gloom in every situation. Someone may ask, "What if you die?" You can declare, "Well, glory to God. I will get to be with Jesus. 2 Corinthians 5:8 says that to be absent from the body is to be present with the Lord. So I'm going to keep on praising the Lord." Just keep that seed in the ground as you go about your business. Make up your mind not to be moved by the problems, adversity, and circumstances that are part of living in a sin-stained world. Don't let all the negativity surrounding you take your focus off God. Keep your focus on the seed, where it belongs.

Back in the early days of our church, our daughter, Anna, had a sty in her eye. Bonnie and I prayed and stood against it, believing that God would heal her. Over the next few days, it got a little bigger. The devil kept whispering, "You'd better go look. You'd better go check. You know, you better go see a doctor. You don't want people to think you're bad parents, do you?" But I refused to look. Every time satan tried to attack, I just praised God. About two weeks after we had first prayed for her, I looked over at Anna during dinner and saw that the sty had vanished. I asked my wife, "When did that happen?" Smiling, Bonnie said, "About three or four days after you prayed."

I had gotten so wrapped up in praising God that I hadn't even gotten to see it go! When I went to sleep at night, I let God produce a harvest from the seed; I didn't get my eyes on the problem. And the Lord took care of it, just like He did one time when I had a small knot on the inside of my lip. It wasn't a life-or-death situation, but it got bad enough that I had to go see a doctor. After he examined me, he said I had a benign tumor. He warned me that if I didn't get it surgically removed, it could keep on growing and expand until it was as big as my head. He told me to make an appointment to see a surgeon. After I'd driven to the surgeon's office, I sat there in the parking lot and thought it over for a while. Finally, I said, "I can either go in there and make an appointment, or we can go on vacation to Florida ... I think I'll go to Florida."

So I stuck the surgeon's card in the glove box and drove

away. Later, when we returned home, I bought several books on healing. I spent the next four days reading, studying, and confessing the Word to my situation. When I prayed on the fourth day, I felt the power of God flowing through me and I just *knew* I would be healed. I had enough seed in the ground to change the situation. About a week later, that tumor disappeared and never returned.

Conquering Problems

That miraculous healing doesn't mean I will never again have any health problems. Living by faith isn't an insurance policy against the enemy's attacks. Earlier in my ministry, I suffered an inner ear problem. It was serious enough that doctors said I wouldn't be able to do much. They told me I would have to learn to live with all kinds of limits and retrain myself to do basic tasks such as walking. They advised me that I would have to give up certain activities and resign myself to a less active lifestyle. I didn't listen. I kept riding my motorcycle, driving my car, and flying on airplanes. I sowed the Word of God into the ground that needed it. I watered it with praise and worship and stood my ground. I relaxed and put my focus on what God said, not what the enemy said.

In other words, I refused to dig up my seed. What happened? Well, I'm still preaching and traveling around the world to proclaim the Word. I know many others who have conquered similar problems. Don't let the devil talk you into digging up your seed. Don't say, "Well, I've got to do something. It's not working. Nothing is happening." Don't do this! Don't talk doubt, fear, or defeat. Don't think it might work for everyone else, but not for you. Don't walk around in a frenzied state, worrying and fretting and wondering why God isn't doing anything in your situation. He will if you will just be patient.

Instead, go ahead and say, "Thank God it's working. I'm not moved by what I see. I'm not moved by what I feel. I'm not moved by these circumstances. I don't care what anyone else is saying. The Word of God is working for me." If you can't say that, get back in the Word and plant it in your heart. Get convinced by the Word; God said it is not devoid of power. It will cause things to happen and make changes in your life. It will produce a harvest and a blessing, but only if you don't dig it up.

chapter 5

Cultivating the Soil

Most of those who lived through the Great Depression of the 1930s are entering their final years on this earth or have already departed it. Soon the memory of those hard times will live on only through history books and newsreels. Those were dreadful times, with unemployment reaching a high of 25 percent. With no government safety net in place, millions were reduced to standing in soup lines or depending on other forms of charity. "Scratching out a living" became more than a trite phrase. Seeing no hope for the future, thousands committed suicide.

"Many families did not have money to buy things, and consumer demand for manufactured goods fell off," writes one historian. "Fewer families were buying new cars or household appliances. People learned to do without new clothing. Many families could not pay their rent. Some young men left home by jumping on railroad cars, in search of any job they could get. Some wondered if the United States was headed for a revolution ... Some farmers became angry and wanted the government to step in to keep farm families in their homes."[1]

The Great Recession that slammed the country in 2008 has drawn comparisons to the Great Depression. Although unemployment reached only 10 percent in recent years, one analyst noted that this statistic failed to take underemployment into account. Three years after the onset of the recession, underemployment stands at 20 percent. In addition, one in six Americans was living off some form of government assistance, more than fifty million were on Medicaid, and ten million more were drawing unemployment benefits.

"I think it is pretty clear that we are in a very precarious economic situation that is highly similar to the Great Depression," wrote *Forbes* contributor David Edwards. "Getting out of this economic situation is going to be very hard. It will take a lot of national pain as our economy transitions from a consumption-based, high-debt, low-growth debtor nation into a manufacturing and exporting nation once again. We will see how that all plays out in the next ten to twenty years."[2]

I find it fascinating how two events separated by nearly eight decades of history can be so similar. In our world, the presence of fear, economic calamity, and lack of supply seem to never go out of style. Back when I was a kid, people used to think if the Soviet Union wasn't around to carry on the Cold War with the United States, we would all be much safer. The Soviet Union collapsed long ago, and the world is more dangerous than ever. And yet, to focus solely on the negative aspects of life is to overlook God's everlasting promise of seedtime and harvest. It still works and it always will as long as there is ground to stand on. Sowing and reaping still occur, just as surely as the sun rises every morning and sets every evening, and just as surely as the seasons change. And it all begins with a seed.

Waiting on the Harvest

Jesus was around at the beginning of time, as evidenced by Genesis: "'Let *Us* make man in *Our* image, according to *Our* likeness; let them have dominion over the fish of the sea, over the birds of the air, and over the cattle, over all the earth and over every creeping thing that creeps on the earth'" (Genesis 1:26; emphasis mine). And yet, Jesus became the Seed of God in this world. Christ didn't come to this earth as a fully grown man, although He easily could have. He came as God's Seed.

We need the same faith in God's seed today that He demonstrated through His Son. I don't give my tithes expecting to go bankrupt. I don't give offerings and contribute to missions and other causes expecting not to have any money left to buy food or gasoline. I expect God to do for me what He said He would do in His Word. He said in Malachi 3:11 that, in response to my giving tithes, He would rebuke the devourer, so that is what I expect Him to do. I act on His Word because I believe that not one single promise of His Word has ever fallen to the ground. It has never lost its power and its ability to perform. I know God watches over His Word. I can trust in Him as my source.

However, as you wait on God's harvest, you must be careful to avoid digging up this seed through doubt and unbelief. The third and fourth chapters of Hebrews discuss how God could not bring the original escapees of slavery in Egypt into the Promised Land because He could not persuade them to believe, act on His Word, and remain consistent. Some of the saddest words in all of Scripture appear in this passage: "Do not harden your hearts as in the rebellion, in the day of trial in the wilderness, where your fathers tested Me, tried Me, and saw My works forty years. Therefore I was angry with that generation, and said, 'They always go astray in their heart, and they have not known My ways.' So I swore in My wrath, 'They shall not enter My rest'" (Hebrews 3:8–11).

Now, these disobedient Israelites started off being with God, praising Him for bringing them out of slavery and then preventing their would-be captors from taking them back into slavery by drowning them in the Red Sea. However, no sooner did things start to look bad in the wilderness than they lost heart and started complaining. They sent spies to look over Canaan; when the group saw some giants, they decided to quit on God, and when they did so, those doubters died on that very spot. Likewise, when you quit on God, that spot marks the exact place where your blessing stops. When you trust in Him, you can enter into His rest, even while you keep laboring. Keep your seed in the ground and it will produce a harvest.

Cultivate the Soil

As you wait for the harvest, you need to do what any good farmer does: cultivate the soil. Let's go back to the parable of the growing seed in Mark: "And He said, 'The kingdom of God is as if a man should scatter seed on the ground, and should sleep by night and rise by day, and the seed should sprout and grow, *he himself does not know how*'" (Mark 4:26–27; emphasis mine). You should draw encouragement from that last phrase. It indicates that you don't have to know everything about God's principle of seedtime and harvest, or even understand how it works. You just have to believe it. Romans 10:9 says that when we combine our mouth's confession of Jesus as Lord with our belief that God raised Him from the dead, we are saved.

Now, there are plenty of things I believe, yet don't quite understand. I don't know how God sitting in heaven can release His anointing to flow through my fingers. And yet I have felt it flow so strongly that I thought it might knock the fingernails off my hand. I have laid hands on people and sensed the tangible power of God flow out of me—and watched them be healed in front of my eyes. I don't know how or why all that works; I just know it does. And I believe it not just because I have experienced it, but also because I have read in the Word that it is possible. I don't know how it is possible to take someone who feels low and, in the next moment, make them feel they are on top of a mountaintop, but I have seen God do it.

I explained earlier that you must plant seed; God won't do it for you. If the Spirit directs you to love somebody and treat them right, then planting a seed is acting on those directions and loving them the way the Bible directs. Proverbs puts it this way: "A man who has friends must himself be friendly" (Proverbs 18:24). This applies to all kinds of areas. For example, if you draw encouragement and instruction from a church, then why not take some of your time and sow it into the work of God's kingdom? Get involved in the life of the church. No matter how small or large a congregation, there is typically a shortage of workers available for getting the job done. Instead of just showing up on Sunday to take in a blessing, why not offer your time and talents to bless others? You may find God amplifying your time by enabling you to accomplish more during every twenty-four hours.

If you feel short on talent, try offering that talent to God and seeing what He does with it. If you say, "I'm suffering from a lack of money," why not start by giving some to God and seeing what He does with it? Anything that helps instruct others in the Word of God is a seed.

Every time you act on the Word, you are sowing a seed. When you give your time to teach Sunday school, care for children, or help operate a food pantry, you are sowing yourself into God's work.

More than Finances

I mention these acts of caring because this key principle goes far beyond money. People mean well, but I think that many too often distort a good teaching from God by associating a harvest solely with what Jesus called *mammon*. Thank God we can believe Him to provide for our needs, but don't make finances the be-all, end-all of life. An overemphasis on finances can reflect an all-consuming worry about provision. Jesus taught us to avoid such folly: "These things dominate the thoughts of unbelievers, but your heavenly Father already knows all your needs. Seek the Kingdom of God above all else, and live righteously, and He will give you everything you need. So don't worry about tomorrow, for tomorrow will bring its own worries. Today's trouble is enough for today" (Matthew 6:32–34 NLT).

If we are seeking God first in all things, we ought to be sowing seeds of love, friendship, time, and obedience to His commands. When the Lord tells us we initiate everything in His kingdom by doing something, He expects us to take action. Don't sit there and gripe and complain, saying, "Well, if somebody came up to me and was friendly, then I would be friends with them." No. That is backward. Luke 6:38 says you must give so that it can be given to you, regardless of what *it* represents. You may be so drowning in credit card debt or so short of money after losing your job that you're lucky to be able to buy a loaf of bread. But you can still give someone a smile, shake their hand, and tell them, "God bless you." Offering encouragement is free!

Besides, chances are you have a few extra dollars but choose to spend them on personal pleasures. Remember, it isn't the amount that makes the difference, but the heart behind the gift. In Mark, right after Jesus warns against following the hypocritical scribes, He praises the poor widow who gives two mites. A mite was a small copper coin only worth a fraction of a penny, so she was giving far less in monetary terms than the rich people who gave considerable sums to the temple. Afterward, "He called His disciples to Himself and said to them, 'Assuredly, I say to you that this poor widow has put in more than all those who have given to the treasury; for they all put in out of their abundance, but she out of her poverty put in all that she had, her whole livelihood'" (Mark 12:43–44).

The widow got a bigger blessing than the rich folks because she sowed generously. She put everything she had in God's hand, and we remember that single act nearly two thousand years later. This demonstrates another truth from Scripture: God will multiply the seed sowed: "Now may He who supplies seed to the sower, and bread for food, supply and multiply the seed you have sown and increase the fruits of your righteousness, while you are enriched in everything for all liberality, which causes thanksgiving through us to God" (2 Corinthians 9:10–11). If you want something to increase in your life, you have to release something out of your life. Sow that seed and God will multiply it.

Earlier in this book, I mentioned how Genesis 1:11 teaches that God said every tree would yield the fruit of the tree with the seed in the fruit, and the seed would yield after its kind. Whatever seed you sow is the harvest you will reap. However, there is a deeper truth from Genesis 1 that you need to understand. Just as God will produce a harvest according to the seed sown, He will not mutate a bad seed into a good harvest. What you sow is what you will reap. Just as you can't expect to get an orange tree from planting an apple seed, God won't take your constant grumbling and complaining and turn you into a leader. He won't take your gossip and telling tales behind someone's back and turn that person into your friend. He won't take your selfishness and turn it into a generous offering. Bad seed won't somehow miraculously turn into good.

Paul put it this way in his letter to the Galatians: "Do not be deceived, God is not mocked; for whatever a man sows, that he will also reap. For he who sows to his flesh will of the flesh reap corruption, but he who sows to the Spirit will of the Spirit reap everlasting life" (Galatians 6:7–8). God can only multiply what you give Him. Seek only superficial relationships and you'll still be longing for close friends. Spend only a few minutes in prayer once or twice a week and you'll still be longing to sense the Holy Spirit working in your life and bringing you closer to the Father. Pay minimal attention to your spouse and you'll reap a loveless, forlorn marriage.

Your Responsibility

Too often, Christians want to escape any responsibility, as if they can sit back and do nothing while God does everything. Not only is that the height of laziness, it is also not Biblical. The Bible teaches that those who follow Christ have a considerable amount of responsibility. Paul taught us "to work out your own salvation with fear and trembling" (Philippians 2:12). Jesus said that "he who does not take his cross and follow after Me is not worthy of Me" (Matthew 10:38). The Bible says we are to regularly attend church, "not forsaking the assembling of ourselves together, as is the manner of some, but exhorting one another, and so much the more as you see the Day approaching" (Hebrews 10:25). We are to be in the Word constantly, too. How do I know that? When satan tried his first cunning temptation on Jesus in the dessert, the Lord replied, "It is written, 'Man shall not live by bread alone, but by every word that proceeds from the mouth of God'" (Matthew 4:4). You are to be a testimony, too, which is taught in Revelation: "And they overcame him [the devil] by the blood of the Lamb and by the word of their testimony, and they did not love their lives to the death" (Revelation 12:11).

The Bible puts a lot of responsibility on you and me, and the Lord says the kingdom of God operates when you initiate action by sowing a seed. So, the first key to seeing a harvest is realizing that God will take anything you give Him and He will increase it. Some people make excuses like, "Well, I didn't give anything during the offering, but God knows my heart." Yes, He does. Such stingy people should be glad it is God who knows rather than those around them. He is more patient, kind, and understanding than others would be if they knew the whole truth and nothing but the truth. Don't expect to be disobedient and then claim that God is going to give you the victory. He will multiply what you gave Him, so when you want to cultivate the soil, the first thing God expects from you is to give. He needs you to place in His hands something to work with.

The second key appears in Mark: "For the earth bringeth forth fruit of herself" (Mark 4:28 KJV). The earth is the soil in which you plant your seed. What is this soil? It is your personal relationship with Jesus Christ. Look to the farmer for a key lesson here. Once he sows his seed, he quits looking at it and turns his eyes to cultivating the soil. Focused on the next important task, he will work the soil until he reaps a harvest.

If we pay too much attention to our seed, keeping our

eyes on the seed and wondering what is wrong with it, why it isn't growing, we allow the devil to fool us. But what does the farmer do? He walks out, looks over the soil, and makes comments like, "I'm gonna have to go ahead and water that ground because it looks a little dry. It won't produce when it's that parched. I'm gonna have to get some water on it." Or, if the summer has been too wet, he knows he has to get some of the water off the ground because the crops are drowning. He protects the soil at all costs.

So, when I say the soil is your relationship with Jesus, it relates to the origin of all men and women; we all came out of the earth. Just as the earth brings forth its own fruit, God works through your relationship with His Son to bring forth spiritual fruit. The Savior taught that "out of the abundance of the heart the mouth speaks" (Matthew 12:34). Men and women bring forth good things out of the abundance of what is in their heart. If they give their heart to God, they will produce a harvest. They are cultivating the soil by developing their walk with Jesus.

Mature Christians recognize that apart from their Lord, they cannot produce any kind of harvest. This is what Jesus taught in John: "I am the vine, you are the branches. He who abides in Me, and I in him, bears much fruit; for without Me you can do nothing. If anyone does not abide in Me, he is cast out as a branch and is withered; and they gather them and throw them into the fire, and they are burned. If you abide in Me, and My words abide in you, you will ask what you desire, and it shall be done for you" (John 15:5–7).

In other words, you have to keep your relationship with God right. Paul starts off the legendary chapter on love, 1 Corinthians 13, by saying that he can give, prophesy, cast down enemies, and be super spiritual. But if he doesn't have love—in other words, if he doesn't have a relationship with an all-loving Lord—then he is nothing. All his power will avail nothing and bring no profit. What Paul is driving at here is that once he has sown his seed, he needs to make sure he keeps the soil in good shape.

This cultivating of the soil is crucial to maintaining your relationship with God. In an era when declining church membership in the West reflects the public's spiritual decline, the eternal destiny of millions is at stake. Too many are fading away because they are allowing the devil to steal the seed before it has a chance to grow. This is a topic I will explore in the final chapter.

chapter 6

Don't Let Go

The history of American business is full of stories of enormous failures, which in some cases cost billions. Does anyone remember Thornburg Mortgage? When it collapsed in 2009, the company was valued at $36 billion. It fell not solely because of subprime loans; Thornburg "specialized in mortgages larger than $417,000 to borrowers with good credit."[1]

Or what about Enron, a company whose name once adorned a major league baseball stadium and that was supposedly a leader in innovative energy trading? When its house of cards came tumbling down, it helped spark passage of federal legislation that set new accounting standards for public-company management, boards of directors, and public accounting firms. Washington Mutual is another firm that was known as a solid savings and loan holding company until regulators seized it after investors withdrew $16.7 billion from WaMu in less than two weeks. Valued at $330 billion when it filed for bankruptcy in September of 2008, it survived only because J.P. Morgan acquired it. That same month, Wall Street investment bank Lehman Brothers went into bankruptcy and ultimately failed when Uncle Sam decided not to bail it out.

The victims in such cases are numerous. Employees of Enron who had put their faith in the company and set up retirement plans with stock holdings saw them wiped out. Investors also lost much, if not all, of the funds they had invested in companies that filed for temporary protection from creditors (known as Chapter 11) but failed to pull out of the tailspin. An article on the website Investopedia notes, "When your company goes bankrupt, there is a very good chance you will not get back the full value of your investment. In fact, there is a chance you won't get anything back. Here is how the SEC summarizes what may happen to stock- and bondholders during Chapter 11:

'During Chapter 11 bankruptcy, bondholders stop receiving interest and principal payments, and stockholders stop receiving dividends. If you are a bondholder, you may receive new stock in exchange for your bonds, new bonds, or a combination of stock and bonds. If you are a stockholder, the trustee may ask you to send back your stock in exchange for shares in the reorganized company. The new shares may be fewer in number and worth less. The reorganization plan spells out your rights as an investor and what you can expect to receive, if anything, from the company.'"

Snatching the Seed

While spectacular business bankruptcies can cost millions of people untold amounts of money, when it comes to failure, there is something even sadder and more spiritually significant. I am talking about people who fail to maintain their grasp on the seed of God's Word and thus fail to cultivate the soil of their heart or to see God bring a harvest that will last for all of eternity.

When Jesus talked in Mark 4 about the sower sowing seed and some of it falling by the wayside, He was prophetic. I have no doubt He foresaw the people in modern-day life who show up occasionally for church to praise God and shout "Hallelujah!" but the day after the service cannot remember what sanctuary they visited. Such fair-weather attendees carry a big fat Bible to church, but never read it, and never get involved in the tough work of helping a church carry out its functions. I see that problem growing worse (at least in America) as we move deeper into the twenty-first century.

I can imagine that, when Jesus referred to the Word falling on stony ground, He was envisioning the shallow Christians who are eager to praise God as long as everything is going well. And yet, at the first sign of trouble or disappointment, they backslide and disappear from church. Because they have no depth in their relationship with God, they are too easily upset, too easily offended, and they are gone too easily. The enemy destroys the seed in their lives because the soil isn't any good.

Jesus also talked about the seed sown among the thorns being choked by weeds and underbrush. You probably know some people like that, who don't have time to develop their relationship with God. They say things like, "Well, I don't know how the pastor expects me to read the Bible with all the things I've got going on in my life. I've got so much to do that everything's just pulling at me. I'm just so busy that I don't have time for God. But I'm saved. I believe in God and I come to church when I can." I would hate to be in such a person's shoes when they stand before Christ on the Day of Judgment.

What makes the difference in your walk with God is not how you start, but how you finish. When someone sponsors a long-distance race, they don't talk about how many runners started, but how many crossed the finish line. They don't keep track of those who gave up and dropped out. God wants you to finish well, too. He wants you to see results produced from your seed. You are part of the root of Christ to become a fruit-bearing vine. Without a strong relationship with Him, you won't produce anything. Without the fruit of His Spirit producing patience and love, you will fade away or succumb to the pressures of the world. Strive to be part of the group that hears the Word, receives it, and acts on it, producing a return by as much as a hundredfold.

Here again, we can learn from the humble farmer. He knows fruit won't sprout overnight. Knowing that a harvest is a process, he gets excited over the appearance of green sprouts, knowing that they signal great crops to come. However, he does not just walk away and expect to return a few months later to gather a harvest. He knows he must get rid of bugs and pests, water the soil, and protect the crops.

Years ago, Bonnie and I got a firsthand lesson in this when we moved back to the farm in Virginia where she grew up. We got all excited about the idea of planting a garden. So we borrowed a neighbor's plow and got the soil churned up and looking good. Then we put in tomato plants and other vegetables and waited. It took only a couple of weeks before I thought, "I don't really want a garden. I want a harvest." A few weeks later, I stopped doing anything. Because I didn't bother to hoe up the soil or to water it, weeds sprouted and the ground cracked during a dry spell.

A neighbor who knew Bonnie's father stopped by one day to see how we were doing. Pointing at the weeds choking the life out of our crops, he asked, "Bonnie, what's that over there? Those weeds over there. That looks like a garden. Is that a garden?"

"Yes," she replied with a nod.

"Well, that's the most pitiful garden I've ever seen in my life."

Being a farmer, he wasn't content to let those weeds choke out our tomatoes and everything else in that plot. He grabbed a hoe, told me to follow him, and made me work with him that night until it was too dark to keep going. Then he returned the next day and made me get out there again until we had cleaned up that garden. It was tough! Bonnie and I had neglected the garden so badly that it wasn't producing anything. But when we cleaned out the weeds, it came back to life. Those plants came alive and we reaped a harvest.

Nourishing Your Relationship

The same is true of your relationship with Jesus. If you don't protect it, the enemy will sow weeds of worry, anxiety, frustration, and aggravation. He will get you to quit because he knows that if he can fill your days and nights with enough junk, the seed won't produce. But when you pluck the weeds out of your life, your garden will produce a great harvest for God, and blessings will flow. When you cultivate your relationship with God, stay on fire, do what He told you to do, and stay in His Word, then—according to Jesus—"By this My Father is glorified, that you bear much fruit; so you will be My disciples" (John 15:8).

In other words, once you plant your seed, stay with

the Word, and see it bear fruit, it is the fruit you produce that will glorify God. It is not you, but He who is glorified. I once had a guy walk up to me and declare in front of a crowd, "Here's a check for ten thousand dollars. I'm sowing this for the kingdom of God." I believe that seed brought glory to the giver. It is the harvest of souls that brings glory to God. The seed is about us, but the harvest is about God; it is trusting God, staying in the Word, and allowing the Lord to be glorified in our lives. Even when it doesn't look like it's working, we must keep praising God, keep praying, keep going, and keep doing. God gets glory because we develop a relationship of trust and faith in Jesus.

When you sow a financial seed as part of putting your finances in God's hands, don't expect that everything will be easy. The work has just begun. You have to have faith that God can bring a supply into your hands. You will have to trust that He will multiply your seed and help you pay your bills. You have to believe that His blessings will come, even though they may not come in the form, the amount, or the way you think they should. You can't trust in God to bring a turnaround in your life if you don't have a relationship with Him. And you won't have that relationship if you don't continually nourish it.

I think this is where most Christians who fade away fall short—not in the planting of the seed, but in failing to cultivate the soil. We get all excited when we plant a seed, but we forget that the miracle will come later, when the earth brings forth the harvest. The miracle is not in the seed, but in your relationship with God. This is what Joshua taught Israel as the nation prepared to cross into the Promised Land: "This Book of the Law shall not depart from your mouth, but you shall meditate in it day and night, that you may observe to do according to all that is written in it. For then you will make your way prosperous, and then you will have good success" (Joshua 1:8).

The guidance and power inherent in this Book, God's Word, shall not depart out of *your* mouth. Not out of your pastor's mouth, or a deacon's, or your best friend's. It is only when you have this Word working in *your* mouth and observe its commands in *your* heart and actions that you will see prosperity and success. You have to meditate on it, think on it, and dwell on it until it gets deep down in your spirit, where it can cultivate your soul. If you're battling stress, financial uncertainty, or depression, you can't pray for just ten minutes a week and expect to emerge triumphant. You can't open your Bible for a few minutes on Sunday morning and expect to be able to confess victory all week long. You have to fill up your life with the Word by putting it in your heart.

Confessing the Word

I still remember what the noted spiritual leader (and founder of Rhema Bible Training College) Kenneth Hagin said while he was alive: "People think because they heard me confess [the Word], they can confess it and they can get the same results. But they can't. If you don't fill your heart full of the Word of God, and fill up the Word of God with the life of God, and confess it, you can't get it. Because it's out of the abundance of the heart that your mouth has to speak, not out of the abundance of your soul. You can know what the Word says but not have a relationship with the Word. If you don't have a relationship with the Word, it won't work for you. To have a relationship with it, you have to spend time with it."

This is why God told Joshua to meditate on the Word day and night. This reflects what Solomon said in his wisdom teachings in Proverbs. He told us not to let his sayings or the Word "depart from your eyes; keep them in the midst of your heart; for they are life to those who find them, and health to all their flesh" (Proverbs 4:21–22). If you can't see your harvest, it may be because you allowed the devil to steal the Word from your eyes. If you keep the Word in front of you, it will show you a harvest. You will be able to see the harvest. When you see yourself healed on the inside, you will eventually see yourself healed on the outside. If you can see your bills paid on the inside, eventually you will see them paid on the outside.

Whatever you have rooted in your heart, you can have in your life. Jesus said that without Him, we can't do it, so what we should be spending time, energy, and effort on is developing our souls and spirits with God's Word so that God can have His way in our lives. We have to cut down some weeds, clean out some junk, and get the garden ready to bloom. That can only happen when you treat God's Word like your life source. You cultivate the soil that will bring a harvest by feeding your spirit and keeping your faith alive. This is what will make your confession powerful, because when you say it, you will believe it––not because you have a knowledge in your head, but because you have a *knowing* in your heart.

This won't come overnight. When you first start meditating on the Word and confessing it for your harvest, you won't necessarily believe. This is a time of great vulnerability. At the very time you are trying to convince yourself to believe God's Word and confess it as if it is so, the devil will wage war against your mind. He will whisper things like, "You hypocrite. You're saying that stuff when you don't really believe it. You know you don't really expect that to happen." You need to reply, "You're right, devil. I don't believe it and don't expect it yet, but the Bible says that if I keep meditating on the Word, reading the Word, and speaking the Word, it will build faith in my life. Your problem is that you know I'm cultivating the soil. I'm getting it ready so I can move on to believing it and saying, 'I'm gonna have it, hallelujah!'"

This may sound like participating in a fantasy or engaging in wishful thinking—but it's not. Let's say you start confessing that you are healed. You may look around and see that nothing's changed. You will still feel bad and the symptoms that you want to go away will still be there. Now, there is a difference between confessing your healing and trying to pretend the illness or whatever the problem is doesn't exist. If your nose is running, you have a 102-degree temperature, and you sound like a foghorn when you talk, confessing your healing doesn't mean you should declare, "I'm not sick." What it does mean is that you know what you are doing. You are sowing a seed and believing that God will bring a harvest.

While you are waiting on the harvest, you will spend time in the Word, and when that Word comes alive, you will believe it. Then, just like a stalk of corn, your body will put out a small blade of healing, followed by a stalk of strength, and then an ear appearing inside the stalk. You will wake up one morning and not have to confess that you are healed anymore—because you are healed! The symptoms will have departed and you can rejoice in the work God has accomplished. Your relationship with Christ has brought forth the harvest that the Word said you could have.

This principle works in every area, whether it be one of physical healing, finance, or personal relationships. Three Scriptures apply here. This is the first:

> For you know the grace of our Lord Jesus Christ, that though He was rich, yet for your sakes He became poor, that you through His poverty might become rich.
>
> —2 Corinthians 8:9

Whenever I read those words, I say, "Thank You, God. I have sowed my seed and as a result, You have redeemed me from the curse of poverty."

With the next verse, I especially like the Amplified Bible's version.

> And God is able to make all grace [every favor and earthly blessing] come to you in abundance, so that you may always and under all circumstances and whatever the need be self-sufficient [possessing enough to require no aid or support and furnished in abundance for every good work and charitable donation].
>
> —2 Corinthians 9:8 AB

I thank God for His grace and favor working on my behalf, just as I do for the promise that appears in Philippians.

> And my God shall supply all your need according to His riches in glory by Christ Jesus.
>
> —Philippians 4:19

This appears at the end of a passage in which Paul praises the Philippian church for its sacrificial giving that supported his gospel mission. When I read about this promise, I rejoice over the certainty of God's provision. After all, there is another often-overlooked verse in this passage in which Paul says of the church's gifts, "Not that I seek the gift, but I seek the fruit that *abounds to your account*" (Philippians 4:17; emphasis mine). Paul is saying that not only will God provide for their needs, He is also such a good bookkeeper that He knows who will accept Jesus as their Savior because of Paul's mission. Also, He will credit those who gave the funds that helped with Paul's travel and other expenses. God is still keeping track today. Your mission gifts are investments in eternity, not money thrown down the drain.

When you get involved in fertilizing your soil with God's Word, enriching the seed with nutrients, and confessing the Word down deep into your heart, you will stop walking around worrying about money. You won't get stressed out over how much money is in your checkbook or how many invoices are stacked up in the bill hopper. You won't worry about what "they" say about your faith or your dependence on God or your lack of desire to wear the latest fashions, drive the newest car, or live in a mansion. You will walk around praising God, knowing that angels are working on your behalf and that you are going over, not under. God will supernaturally work on your behalf to bring the harvest from your seed.

So keep cultivating the soil. Strengthen your relationship with the Lord by strengthening your relationship with His Word. When you abide in Christ, and His words abide in you, you will produce much fruit and your Father will be glorified. Such is the miracle of the seed. It grows where people can't see it, bears fruit in ways humans can't logically understand, and brings a glorious, eternal harvest.

Notes

Chapter 1

1. Keith Swenson and David Catchpoole, "After devastation ... the recovery," Creation Ministries International, http://creation.com/after-devastation-the-recovery.
2. Statistical Research on Stewardship, Francis Schaeffer Institute of Church Leadership, http://biblicalstewardship.net/statistical-research-on-stewardship/.

Chapter 2

1. Ellen Goodstein, "8 lottery winners who lost their millions," Bankrate.com, http://www.wastedyourtime.com/rub-off/lostwinners.htm.
2. Ibid.

Chapter 3

1. Warren Richey, "Did China steal U.S. corn? Six charged with digging up bioengineered seed," *Christian Science Monitor*, Dec. 19, 2013 http://www.csmonitor.com/USA/Justice/2013/1219/Did-China-steal-US-corn-Six-charged-with-digging-up-bioengineered seed.

2. Michael R. Briggs, "Updating the King James: Launching a new Bible translation in the spirit of the venerable version," *Christian Retailing*, September 2014, 16.

Chapter 4

1. Eddie Wren, "The Dangers of Traveling by Road in Other Countries," Advanced Drivers of America, 2010, http://www.advanceddrivers.com/info_80002.htm.

Chapter 5

1. "The Great Depression Hits Farm and Cities in the 1930s," Iowa Pathways, Iowa Public Television, http://www.iptv.org/iowapathways/mypath.cfm?ounid=ob_000064.
2. David Edwards, "How Does The Current Recession Compare to The Great Depression?" November 8, 2011, *Forbes* online, http://www.forbes.com/sites/quora/2011/11/08/how-does-the-current-economic-recession-compare-to-the-great-depression/.

Chapter 6

1. "An Overview of Corporate Bankruptcy," http://www.investopedia.com/articles/01/120501.asp.

Printed in the United States
By Bookmasters